EVERYDAY

A CASUAL, MODERN HAND-KNIT COLLECTION

11 designs by JEN GEIGLEY

PHOTOGRAPHY by JOELLE BLANCHARD and JOEY LEAMING

Design & Pattern Writing | Jen Geigley
Photography | Joelle Blanchard, Joey Leaming
Design, Layout & Illustrations | Jen Geigley
Models | Joelle Blanchard, Chantell Moody, Valerie Sanders
Technical Editing | Stefanie Goodwin-Ritter
Sample Knitting | Rebecca Huben, Nichole McDowell
Location | Des Moines, Iowa

Everyday: A casual, modern hand-knit collection

Wholesale Ordering Information
Deep South Fibers
www.deepsouthfibers.com

Library of Congress Control Number: 2016916557
ISBN: 978-0-9965805-3-3 paperback
ISBN: 978-0-9965805-4-0 ebook

((((((●
MOON PHASE PUBLICATIONS

www.MoonPhasePublications.com

CRA015000
Crafts & Hobbies | Needlework | Knitting

10 9 8 7 6 5 4 3 2 1

C O N T E N T S

INTRODUCTION

Find something special in your everyday. I knit every day. Or nearly every day. Knitting has become an integral part of my existence – like music; like breathing. Knitting before bed is my nightcap, my zen. Knitting while I travel is one of my most favorite things to do. If you are a knitter, I know you feel the same. This hobby is a fundamental part of our everyday.

This book has something for everyone – new knitters may find their first sweater in these pages and experienced knitters will enjoy the combination of an advanced knitting stitch (like the Lateral Braid) with modern shapes. These pieces will appeal to the knitter who has an appreciation for fashion.

I invite you to discover a collection of hand knits that are casual, comfortable and truly fun to knit and wear. The modern silhouettes of the tanks and sweaters in this book will work their way into every season of your wardrobe, on their own or as layering pieces. Chunky, bulkier yarns round out this collection with a cozy range of accessories to get you through the colder months.

Form or function? I don't think you have to choose. When you are a knitter, you can have it all. Knit. Wear. Live life to the fullest. Make it just the way you want it. Make it your own. Fill your life with things that look cool and are easy to wear in your everyday.

– Jen Geigley

THE COLLECTION

ERIS

EQUINOX

LANEY

THE PATTERNS

GWEN

DESIGN NOTES

Gwen is a gorgeously soft scarf/cowl that's easy to wear. Stay cozy and warm in this accessory that you'll want to wear with everything. Slip the cowl over your head like a turtleneck and throw one of scarf tails over your shoulder. The cowl section is worked seamlessly in the round, then the scarf is knit flat and seamed to the cowl.

SIZES

One size

FINISHED MEASUREMENTS

Cowl – 30 inch circumference (unstretched) and 9 inches from top to bottom
Scarf – 8.5 inches wide, 68 inches long

YARN

Spud & Chloë by Blue Sky Fibers Outer in Carbon
(Super bulky; 65% superwash wool, 35% organic cotton; 60 yds per 100g hank)
5 hanks
300 yards

NEEDLES

US 15 (10 mm) 24 inch circular needles
(or size needed to obtain gauge)

NOTIONS

Tapestry needle
Stitch Marker

GAUGE

4 inches = 8 sts and 10 rows in single rib on US 15 (10 mm) needles

STITCH GUIDE

Single Rib - in the round:
All rnds: *K1, p1, rep from *.

Single Rib - worked flat:
Row 1: *K1, p1, rep from *.
Row 2: *P1, k1, rep from *.

ABBREVIATIONS

CO – cast on
BO – bind off
k – knit
st(s) – stitch(es)
rnd – round
beg – beginning
inc – increase
p – purl
pm – place marker
pw – purl wise
rep – repeat
rnd – round
st st – stockinette stitch

DIRECTIONS

Cowl section

Using long-tail method on US 15 needles, CO 60 sts. Join to work in the round, taking care not to twist sts. PM to mark beginning of round.

Work Single Rib stitch patt in the round until piece measures 9 inches from CO edge.

Next rnd: BO in pattern, loosely.

Scarf section

Using long-tail method on US 15 needles, CO 17 sts.

Work flat in Single Rib stitch patt for 10 rows.

Beg scarf pattern, slipping all slipped sts PW (with yarn held in front).

1. K4, sl1, k1, sl1, p3, sl1, k1, sl1, k4.

2. K3, p across to last 3 sts, k3.

3. K5, sl1, k1, p3, k1, sl1, k5.

4. K3, p across to last 3 sts, k3.

Rep rows 1-4 until piece measures 64 inches from CO edge.

Work Single Rib stitch patt for 9 rows.

BO all sts in pattern, loosely.

FINISHING

Cut yarn, leaving a 6-8 in tail. Using tapestry needle, weave in ends.

Lay cowl flat and seam side edge of the scarf around entire bottom edge of the cowl, leaving one scarf end shorter than the other. (See schematic.)

BLOCKING

Lay out garment and shape to desired shape and dimensions. Gently spritz with water in a spray bottle until damp, but not soaking wet. Allow to dry completely.

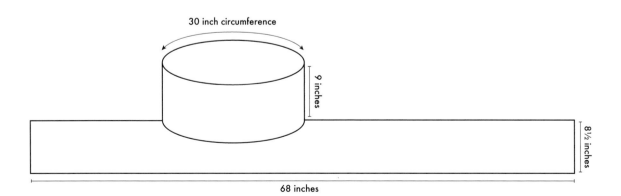

30 inch circumference

9 inches

8½ inches

68 inches

LEO

DESIGN NOTES

Leo is the ultimate super scarf and is quite enjoyable to knit. Make a statement in this oversized piece and stay cozy this winter. Knit flat using a stitch pattern that's easy to remember, you'll be adding fringe and wearing this fantastically cool scarf in no time.

SIZES
One size

FINISHED MEASUREMENTS
11 x 112 inches (not including fringe)

YARN
Briggs and Little Country Roving in Sheep's Grey (Super bulky; 100% wool; 155 yds per 8 oz ball)
2.5 balls
380 yds

NEEDLES
US 19 (16 mm) needles
(or size needed to obtain gauge)

NOTIONS
Tapestry needle

GAUGE
4 inches = 5 sts and 8 rows in 1x1 rib on US 19 needles, unblocked

STITCH GUIDE
1x1 Rib
Row 1: *K1, p1, rep from * to end of row.
Row 2: *P1, k1, rep from * to end of row.

Roman Stripe Pattern
Row 1 (RS): K1, *yo, k1; rep from * to last st, k1.
Row 2 (WS): K1, p to last st, k1.
Row 3: K1, *k2tog; rep from * to last st, k1.
Rows 4 + 5: K1, *yo, k2tog, rep from * to last st, k1.
Rows 6-9: K all sts.

ABBREVIATIONS
CO – cast on
BO – bind off
beg – beginning
k – knit
k2tog – knit 2 stitches together
st(s) – stitch(es)
sl 1 kw – slip 1 knitwise
p – purl
rep – repeat
RS – right side
WS – wrong side
yo – yarn over

DIRECTIONS

Using long-tail method on US 19 needles, CO 16 sts.

Work in 1x1 Rib stitch for 10 rows.

Next row: Begin working in Roman Stripe pattern.

Repeat pattern until piece measures 104 inches from CO edge.

Next row: Work in 1x1 Rib stitch for 9 rows.

BO in pattern, loosely. Break yarn.

FINISHING

Using tapestry needle, weave in ends.

To add fringe, cut a piece of cardboard that is 8 inches long. Wind yarn loosely several times around cardboard. Use scissors to cut yarn across one end of the wrapped cardboard. Hold 5 strands of fringe together, and fold them in half. Starting at one corner of the BO or CO edge, use a crochet hook (or your fingers) to pull folded end of fringe from the RS to the WS of project. Pull loose ends through the loop of the folded section. Pull into a knot. Continue across project, spacing the fringe knots evenly.

BLOCKING

I do not recommend blocking this particular yarn/garment. If blocking is needed, lay out garment and shape to desired shape and dimensions. Gently spritz with water in a spray bottle until damp, but not soaking wet. Allow to dry completely.

CERES

DESIGN NOTES

Ceres is an easy, breezy racerback tank that is oh-so-soft and lovely to throw on. With 2 inches of positive ease, it is meant to fit loosely. This top is first worked in the round for the body, then flat in stockinette stitch with garter stitch edging. The only seams are on the shoulders.

SIZES

XS (S, M, L, XL)
To Fit Bust: 34 (38, 42, 46, 50) inches with 2 inches positive ease

FINISHED BUST MEASUREMENTS

36 (40, 44, 48, 52) inches

YARN

Manos Del Uruguay Silk Blend in Black (DK; 30% silk and 70% extrafine merino; 150 yards per 1.75 oz hank)
5 (5, 6, 6, 7) hanks
750 (750, 900, 900, 1050) yards

NEEDLES

US 8 (5 mm) 24 inch circular needles
(or size needed to obtain gauge)

NOTIONS

Stitch marker
Tapestry needle
Stitch holder or scrap yarn

GAUGE

4 inches = 20 sts and 28 rows in St st on size 8 (5 mm) needles

STITCH GUIDE

Garter Stitch (worked in the round)
Round 1: P all sts.
Round 2: K all sts.

Stockinette Stitch (worked in the round)
K all sts.

Stockinette Stitch (worked flat):
Row 1 (RS): K all sts.
Row 2 (WS): P all sts.

ABBREVIATIONS

CO – cast on
BO – bind off
k – knit
k2tog – k 2 sts together (1 st dec)
kf&b – knit into front and back of stitch (1 st incr)
st(s) – stitch(es)
rnd – round
beg – beginning
dec – decrease
incr – increase
p – purl
p2tog – p 2 sts together (1 st dec)
pm – place marker
rep – repeat
rem – remain
rnd – round
RS – right side
sl – slip
sm – slip marker
ssk – slip slip knit (1 st dec)
WS – wrong side

DIRECTIONS

Using long-tail method and US 8 (5 mm) needles, CO 180 (200, 220, 240, 260) sts. Join for knitting in the rnd and PM, taking care not to twist sts.

Work 5 rnds total in Garter Stitch, beginning and ending with a purl row.

Switch to Stockinette Stitch and work until piece measures 15 (15, 16, 16, 17) inches from CO edge.

Divide front and back

BO 5 (5, 5, 6, 6) sts. K 85 (95, 105, 115, 125) sts. BO 5 (5, 5, 6, 6) sts. K 85 (95, 105, 115, 125) sts around to marker. 170 (190, 210, 228, 248) sts remain - 85 (95, 105, 114, 124) sts each for front and back.

Front and back will be worked separately; place 85 (95, 105, 114, 124) sts on holders or scrap yarn for front; rem 85 (95, 105, 114, 124) sts on needles will be worked for back.

BACK (work flat)

Beginning on WS, turn work and BO 5 sts at beg of next 2 rows. 75 (85, 95, 104, 114) sts rem.

Beginning on WS, BO 4 sts at beg of next 4 rows. 59 (69, 79, 88, 98) sts rem.

Beginning on WS, BO 3 sts at beg of next 3 rows, 3 times total. 32 (42, 52, 61, 71) sts rem.

Beginning on RS, BO 2 sts at beg of next 2 rows, 0 (2, 4, 6, 8) times total. 32 (34, 36, 37, 39) sts rem.

Dec Row (RS): K1, ssk, k to last 3 sts, k2tog, k1.
Next Row (WS): P all sts.

Repeat above 2 rows a total of 5 (6, 6, 6, 7) times. 22 (22, 24, 25, 25) sts rem.

Continue in Stockinette Stitch until armhole measures 8 (8, 8, 9, 9) inches, ending on WS row.

Next row (RS): K1, kf&b, k to last 2 sts, kf&b, k1. 24 (24, 26, 27, 27) sts.
Next row (WS): P all sts.
CO 2 sts at beg of next 2 (2, 3, 4, 5) rows. 28 (28, 32, 35, 27) sts.
CO 3 sts at beg of next 2 (2, 2, 3, 3) rows. 34 (34, 38, 44, 46) sts.
CO 4 sts at beg of next 3 (4, 4, 4, 4) rows. 46 (50, 54, 60, 62) sts.
Work until armhole measures 10 (10, 11, 11, 12) inches, ending with WS row.

Next row (RS): K 15 sts, join a second ball of yarn and BO center 16 (20, 24, 30, 32) sts. K to end of row - 30 sts rem total, 15 sts for each strap.

Knit both straps in Stockinette Stitch at the same time using separate balls of yarn. Work until armhole measures 12 (12, 12, 13, 14) inches, ending on WS.
BO each strap.

FRONT (work flat)

Transfer 85 (95, 105, 114, 124) held sts to needles and join yarn to begin working on RS. BO 4 sts at beg of next 2 rows. 77 (87, 97, 106, 116) sts rem.

BO 2 sts at beg of next 3 rows. 71 (81, 91, 100, 110) sts rem.

Dec Row (WS): K1, p2tog, p to last 3 sts, p2tog, p1. 69 (79, 89, 98, 108) sts rem.

Beginning on RS, work even in Stockinette Stitch until armhole measures 8 (9, 9, 10, 11) inches. End on WS.

Next row (RS): K 27 (32, 37, 41, 46) sts, join a second ball of yarn and BO center 15 (15, 15, 16, 16) sts. K to end of row - 54 (64, 74, 82, 92) sts rem total, 27 (32, 37, 41, 46) sts for each strap.

Both straps will be worked in Stockinette Stitch at the same time using separate balls of yarn, starting with a WS row.

Begin decreases:
Next Row (RS): K1, ssk, k to last 3 sts, k2tog, k1.
Next Row (WS): P all sts.

Work the above two rows 4 (4, 5, 6, 7) times total. 19 (24, 27, 29, 32) sts rem.

Neck Decrease Row (RS): On first strap, k to last 3 sts, k2tog, k1. On second strap, k1, ssk, k to end.
Next Row (WS): P all sts.

Work the above two rows 4 (9, 12, 14, 17) times total. 15 sts rem on each strap.

Work until armhole measures 12 (12, 12, 13, 14) inches or until front straps line up with back straps, ending on WS. BO each strap.

SEAMING

Seam shoulder straps using shoulder seam stitch - or - sew a simple seam with the edges exposed, as shown in the sample.

EDGING

Arm openings

Starting at underarm, pick up and knit 110 sts around arm opening.

Work 5 rnds total in Garter Stitch, beginning and ending with a purl row.

BO all sts.

Repeat for second arm opening.

Neck opening

Starting at shoulder seam, pick up and knit 90 sts around neck opening.

Work 5 rnds total in Garter Stitch, beginning and ending with a purl row.

BO all sts using Jeny Staiman's Surprisingly Stretchy Bind-Off, or your favorite stretchy bind off method.

FINISHING

Using tapestry needle, weave in ends.

BLOCKING

Soak using your favorite no-rinse wash in lukewarm water for 15-20 minutes, gently lay garment out and shape. Dry flat.

FRONT

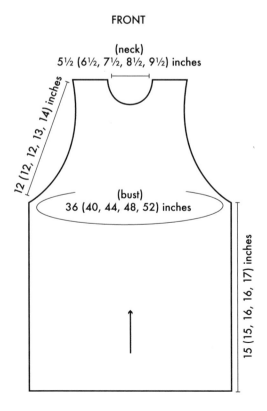

(neck)
5½ (6½, 7½, 8½, 9½) inches

12 (12, 12, 13, 14) inches

(bust)
36 (40, 44, 48, 52) inches

15 (15, 16, 16, 17) inches

BACK

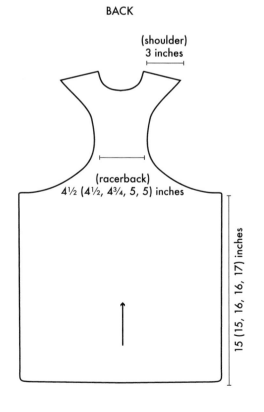

(shoulder)
3 inches

(racerback)
4½ (4½, 4¾, 5, 5) inches

15 (15, 16, 16, 17) inches

ERIS

DESIGN NOTES

Treat yourself to cashmere and cozy up with this super soft cowl on a chilly day. This cowl has two slits – but don't worry, you'll stay warm. Eris is worked seamlessly in the round and knits up quickly. Knit one for yourself, then knit one for someone you love.

SIZES
One size

FINISHED MEASUREMENTS
28 inch circumference and 18 inches from top to bottom

YARN
Lux Adorna Knits 100% Cashmere Bulky in Kitten
(Bulky; 100% Cashmere; 80 yds per 2.68 oz hank)
3 hanks
240 yards

NEEDLES
US 11 (8 mm) 24 inch circular needles
(or size needed to obtain gauge)

NOTIONS
Tapestry needle
Stitch Marker

GAUGE
4 inches = 11 sts and 17 rows in St st on US 11 (8 mm) needles

STITCH GUIDE
Single Rib
All rnds: *K1, p1, rep from *.

Stockinette Stitch
All rnds: K all sts.

ABBREVIATIONS
CO – cast on
BO – bind off
k – knit
st(s) – stitch(es)
rnd – round
beg – beginning
inc – increase
p – purl
pm – place marker
rep – repeat
rnd – round
st st – stockinette stitch

DIRECTIONS

Using long-tail method on US 11 needles, CO 74 sts. Join to work in the round, taking care not to twist sts. PM to mark beginning of rnd.

Work Single Rib stitch patt for 5 rnds total.

Begin working in Stockinette Stitch until piece measures 6 inches from CO edge.

Next rnd: BO 15 sts, k to end of rnd.

Next rnd: CO 15 sts, k to end of rnd.

Work in Stockinette Stitch until piece measures 6 inches from slit you just created.

Next rnd: K17 sts, BO 15 sts, k to end of rnd.

Next rnd: K17 sts, CO 15 sts, k to end of rnd.

Work in Stockinette Stitch until piece measures 4 1/2 inches from slit you just created.

Work Single Rib stitch patt for 5 rnds total.

BO all sts in pattern, loosely.

FINISHING

Cut yarn, leaving a 6-8 inch tail. Using tapestry needle, weave in ends.

BLOCKING

I do not recommend blocking this particular yarn/garment. If blocking is needed, lay out garment and shape to desired shape and dimensions. Gently spritz with water in a spray bottle until damp, but not soaking wet. Allow to dry completely.

JESSA

DESIGN NOTES

This fantastically chunky top can be knitted in cropped or regular length. Jessa can be worn as-is or over a long-sleeved shirt as an added layer of warmth. This boxy top is knitted from the bottom up. The body is worked seamless in the round, then the front + back are knit flat and then seamed at shoulders.

SIZES

To Fit Bust: 34 (38, 42, 46, 50, 54) inches

FINISHED MEASUREMENTS

Finished Bust Circumference: 34.5 (38.5, 42.5, 46.5, 50.5, 54.5) inches

YARN

Blue Sky Fibers Bulky in Curry (Bulky; 50% alpaca and 50% wool; 45 yards per 100 g hank)

Cropped Length
5 (6, 7, 7, 8, 9) hanks
225 (270, 270, 315, 360, 405) yards

Regular Length
6 (7, 8, 9, 11, 12) hanks
270 (315, 360, 405, 495, 540) yards

NEEDLES

US 19 (16 mm) 24 inch circular needles
(or size needed to obtain gauge)

US 17 (12 mm) 24 inch circular needles for picking up stitches

NOTIONS

Tapestry needle
Stitch Marker

GAUGE

4 inches = 6 sts and 8 rows in St st on size 19 (16 mm) needles

ABBREVIATIONS

CO – cast on

BO – bind off

k – knit

k2tog – knit 2 sts together (1 stitch decreased)

st(s) – stitch(es)

rnd – round

beg – beginning

dec – decrease

inc – increase

p – purl

p2tog – purl 2 sts together (1 stitch decreased)

pm – place marker

rep – repeat

rem – remain

rnd – round

RS – right side

st st – stockinette stitch

sl – slip

sm – slip marker

WS – wrong side

CROPPED LENGTH

(neck)
10 (11, 12, 13, 14, 15) inches

(shoulder)
3¾ (4, 4, 5, 7) inches

(arm opening)
9½ (10, 10½, 11, 11½, 12) inches

3½
inches

(bust)
34 (38, 42, 46, 50, 54) inches

10 (10, 11, 12, 12, 13) inches

REGULAR LENGTH

(neck)
10 (11, 12, 13, 14, 15) inches

(shoulder)
3¾ (4, 4, 5, 7) inches

(arm opening)
9½ (10, 10½, 11, 11½, 12) inches

3½
inches

(bust)
34 (38, 42, 46, 50, 54) inches

17, (17, 17½, 18, 18½, 19) inches

DIRECTIONS

Using long-tail method and US 19 (16 mm) needles, CO 52 (58, 64, 70, 76, 82) sts. Join to work in the round, taking care not to twist sts. PM to mark beginning of round.

Work in Single Rib Stitch for 4 rnds total.

Begin working in Stockinette Stitch until piece measures 17, (17, 17.5, 18, 18.5, 19) inches for regular length, or 10 (10, 11, 12, 12, 13) inches for cropped length from CO edge. End after WS rnd.

Transfer last 26 (29, 32, 35, 38, 41) sts of rnd to stitch holders or scrap yarn to be worked for Front. 26 (29, 32, 35, 38, 41) sts rem on needles for Back.

BACK (work flat)

Next row (RS): K 26 (29, 32, 35, 38, 41) sts.

Next row (WS): Turn work and, slipping first st, p to end of row.

Slipping first st of every row, cont working in Stockinette Stitch until arm opening measures 9.5 (10, 10.5, 11, 11.5, 12) inches.

At beg of next 2 rows, BO 5 (5, 6, 7, 7, 8) sts. 16 (19, 20, 21, 24, 25) sts rem.

BO rem sts for back of neck.

FRONT (work flat)

Transfer held 26 (29, 32, 35, 38, 41) sts to needles and work as for back until arm openings measure 7.5 (8, 8.5, 9, 9.5, 10) inches, ending with WS row.

With RS facing, k 8 (10, 10, 12, 12, 13) sts.

Join new yarn and BO center 10 (9, 12, 11, 14, 15) for crew neck.

Work to end of row.

8 (10, 10, 12, 12, 13) sts rem on each side.

Work each side at the same time using separate balls of yarn.

Next row (WS): P to last 2 sts, p2tog across first set of sts; P2tog, p to end across second set of sts. 7 (9, 9, 11, 11, 12) sts rem each side.

Next row (RS): K to last 2 sts, k2tog across first set of sts; K2tog, k to end across second set of sts. 6 (8, 8, 10, 10, 11) sts rem each side.

Purl across both sets of sts.

Next row (RS): K to last 2 sts, k2tog across first set of sts; K2tog, k to end across second set of sts 1 (1, 1, 2, 2, 2) more times. 5 (7, 7, 8, 8, 9) sts rem on each side.

Work even until shoulders on front measure the same as the back.

BO rem sts.

Seaming

Seam shoulder using shoulder seam stitch, or sew a simple seam with the edges exposed.

Edging

Arm openings

With smaller needles and right side facing and starting at underarm, pick up and knit 28 (30, 32, 32, 34, 36) sts around arm opening.

Next rnd: Work in Single Rib Stitch in the round for 7 rnds total.

BO in pattern, loosely.

Repeat for second arm opening.

Neck opening

With smaller needles, right side facing and starting at right shoulder, pick up and knit 30 (32, 36, 38, 42, 44) sts around neck opening.

Next rnd: Work in Single Rib Stitch in the round for 7 rnds total.

BO in pattern, loosely.

FINISHING

Using tapestry needle, weave in ends.

BLOCKING

I do not recommend blocking this particular yarn/garment. If blocking is needed, lay out garment and shape to desired shape and dimensions. Gently spritz with water in a spray bottle until damp, but not soaking wet. Allow to dry completely.

CHILL

DESIGN NOTES

Chill in this pair of super bulky, cozy fingerless mitts. Keep your hands warm and set your fingers free. These mitts are super quick to knit and are worked in the round.

SIZES

One size

FINISHED MEASUREMENTS

4.5 x 7 inches (9" circumference)

YARN

Wool and the Gang Crazy Sexy Wool in Space Black
(Super Bulky, 100% Peruvian wool; 87 yards per 200 g ball)
1 ball
87 yards

NEEDLES

US 15 (10 mm) DPNs
(or size needed to obtain gauge)

NOTIONS

Stitch marker
Tapestry needle

GAUGE

4 inches = 8 sts and 12 rows in St st on size 15 (10 mm) needles, unblocked

STITCH GUIDE

Single Rib (worked in the round)
All rnds: *P1, k1, rep from *.

Seed Stitch
Row 1: *K1, p1; rep from * to end of rnd.
Row 2: *P1, k1; rep from * to end of rnd.
Rep rows 1 and 2 for pattern.

Stockinette Stitch (worked in the round)
All rnds: K all sts.

ABBREVIATIONS

CO – cast on
BO – bind off
k – knit
st(s) – stitch(es)
rnd – round
beg – beginning
dec – decrease
est – established
inc – increase
m – marker
m1r – make 1 right
m1l – make 1 left
p – purl
patt – pattern
pm – place marker
pu – pick up
rep – repeat
rem – remaining
rnd(s) – round
RS – right side
st(s) – stitch(es)
sl – slip
sm – slip marker
WS – wrong side

DIRECTIONS

Using long-tail method and US 15 (10 mm) needles, CO 18 sts. Distribute sts on 3 DPNs, join for working in the round and PM, taking care not to twist sts.

Right Mitt

Work Single Rib stitch pattern for 5 rnds total.

Next rnd: K2, work in Seed Stitch for 4 sts, then work in Stockinette Stitch until end of rnd. Work in established patt for 4 more rnds.

Thumb Gusset

Rnd 1: Work across first 9 sts in established patt, PM, m1r, k1, m1l, PM, k to end of rnd. 20 sts.

Rnd 2: Work across first 9 sts in established patt, sl m, work in Stockinette Stitch to next marker, sl m, then work in Stockinette Stitch until end of rnd.

Rnd 3: Work across first 9 sts in established patt, sl m, m1r, k3, m1l, sl m, then work in Stockinette Stitch until end of rnd. 22 sts.

Rnd 4: Work across first 9 sts in established patt, sl m, work in Stockinette Stitch to next marker, sl m, then work in Stockinette Stitch until end of rnd.

Rnd 5: Work across first 9 sts in established patt to marker, place next 5 sts on waste yarn or holder for thumb. Using backward loop method, CO 1 st, then work in Stockinette Stitch until end of rnd. 18 sts.

Hand/Fingers

Work 2 rnds in established patt.

Next rnd: Work Single Rib stitch pattern for 4 rnds. BO in pattern.

Thumb

Remove sts from waste yarn or holder and distribute on DPNs.

PU 1 st from area above thumb hole. (6 sts)

Work in Stockinette Stitch for 4 rnds.

BO.

Left Mitt

Work Single Rib stitch pattern for 5 rnds total.

Next rnd: K7, work in Seed Stitch for 4 sts, then work in Stockinette Stitch until end of rnd. Work in established patt for 4 more rnds.

Thumb Gusset

Rnd 1: Work across first 3 sts in established patt, PM, m1r, k1, m1l, PM, k to end of rnd. 20 sts.

Rnd 2: Work across first 3 sts in established patt, sl m, work in Stockinette Stitch to next marker, sl m, then work in established patt until end of rnd.

Rnd 3: Work across first 3 sts in established patt, sl m, m1r, k3, m1l, sl m, then work in established patt until end of rnd. 22 sts.

Rnd 4: Work across first 3 sts in established patt, sl m, work in Stockinette Stitch to next marker, sl m, then work in established patt until end of rnd.

Rnd 5: Work across first 3 sts in established patt to marker, place next 5 sts on waste yarn or holder for thumb. Using backward loop method, CO 1 st, then work in established patt until end of rnd. 18 sts.

Hand/Fingers

Work 2 rnds in established patt.

Next rnd: Work Single Rib stitch pattern for 4 rnds. BO in pattern.

Thumb

Remove sts from waste yarn or holder and distribute on DPNs. PU 1 st from area above thumb hole. (6 sts)

Work in Stockinette Stitch for 4 rnds.

BO.

FINISHING

Using tapestry needle, weave in ends.

BLOCKING

I do not recommend blocking this particular yarn/garment. If blocking is needed, lay out garment and shape to desired shape and dimensions. Gently spritz with water in a spray bottle until damp, but not soaking wet. Allow to dry completely.

AURA

DESIGN NOTES

Aura is the perfect winter hat with a panel of seed stitch to add a bit of texture. Worked in the round, it knits up quickly and makes a fantastic gift. Wear yours every day.

SIZES
One size

FINISHED MEASUREMENTS
19 inches circumference and 10 inches high
(before pom-pom)

YARN
Wool and the Gang Crazy Sexy Wool in Space Black
(Super Bulky, 100% Peruvian wool; 87 yards per 200 g ball)
1 ball
87 yards

NEEDLES
US 15 (10 mm) 16" circular needle
(or size needed to obtain gauge)

US 15 (10 mm) DPNs
(or size needed to obtain gauge)

NOTIONS
Stitch marker
Tapestry needle

GAUGE
4 inches = 8 sts and 12 rows in St st on size 15 (10 mm) needles, unblocked

STITCH GUIDE
Single Rib (worked in the round)
All rnds: *P1, k1, rep from *.

Seed Stitch
Row 1: *K1, p1; rep from *.
Row 2: *P1, k1; rep from *.
Rep rows 1 and 2 for pattern.

Stockinette Stitch (worked in the round)
All rnds: K all sts.

ABBREVIATIONS
CO – cast on
BO – bind off
k – knit
st(s) – stitch(es)
rnd – round
beg – beginning
dec – decrease
est – established
m – marker
m1r – make 1 right
m1l – make 1 left
p – purl
patt – pattern
pm – place marker
pu – pick up
rep – repeat
rem – remaining
rnd(s) – round
RS – right side
st(s) – stitch(es)
sl – slip
sm – slip marker
WS – wrong side

DIRECTIONS

Using long-tail method and US 15 (10 mm) needles, CO 36 sts. Join for working in the round and PM, taking care not to twist sts.

Work Single Rib stitch pattern for 10 rnds total.

Begin working in pattern: Work Seed Stitch across first 8 sts of rnd, pm, then work in Stockinette Stitch until end of rnd.

Rep this patt, slipping marker as you come to it, until piece measures 7 inches from CO edge.

Dec Rnd: Work seed Stitch across first 8 sts of rnd, sl m, K to last 2 sts or rnd, k2tog. (35 sts rem)

Shape Crown

Maintaining pattern as much as possible (you will be one st off on Seed Stitch section), shape crown as follows. Switch to DPNs when necessary.

Crown Decrease Rnd 1: *K3, k2tog, rep from * to end of rnd. (28 sts rem)

Next Rnd: K all sts in established patt.

Crown Decrease Rnd 2: *K2, k2tog, rep from * to end of rnd. (21 sts rem)

Next Rnd: K all sts in established patt.

Crown Decrease Rnd 3: *K1, k2tog, rep from * to end of rnd. (14 sts rem)

Next Rnd: K all sts in established patt.

FINISHING

Cut yarn, leaving a 6-8 in tail. Using tapestry needle, thread rem sts onto tail. Pull tight and secure, weave in ends.

POM-POM (optional)

Cut out two cardboard doughnuts 5 inches in diameter to make optional pom-pom. Sandwich a piece of yarn 8 inches long between the two layers. Cut a slit in both pieces of cardboard from outer edge to inner circle. Wind yarn over the doughnut, around and around, working the yarn through the center hole on each pass. Insert a scissors between the two layers of the form and cut the strands of pom-pom yarn where they cross over the outer edge of the circles. Pull up the center yarn tightly. Tie the center yarn in a tight knot. Fluff the pom-pom into shape and trim any stray ends. Use the center 8 inch piece of yarn to attach pom-pom to top of hat.

BLOCKING

I do not recommend blocking this particular yarn/garment. If blocking is needed, lay out garment and shape to desired shape and dimensions. Gently spritz with water in a spray bottle until damp, but not soaking wet. Allow to dry completely.

MOONSTONE

DESIGN NOTES

Moonstone is a super soft top, knit in garter stitch which really shows off the hand-dyed variances in this gorgeous yarn. A small side slit near the bottom hem on the front adds a little bit of personality to this top. Wear it alone or as a layering piece. Moonstone is worked flat and seamed.

SIZES

XS (S, M, L, XL)
To Fit Bust: 36 (40, 44, 48, 52) inches

FINISHED BUST MEASUREMENTS

36 (40, 44, 48, 52) inches

YARN

Manos Del Uruguay Maxima Fair Trade Merino in Kohl
(Worsted; 100% merino wool; 219 yards per 200 g hank)
4 (5, 6, 7, 7) hanks
876 (1095, 1314, 1533, 1533) yards

NEEDLES

US 8 (5 mm) 24 inch circular needles
(or size needed to obtain gauge)

US 7 (4.5 mm) 24 inch circular needles
(for picking up stitches)

NOTIONS

Stitch marker
Tapestry needle

GAUGE

4 inches = 17 sts and 35 rows in Garter Stitch on US 8 (5 mm) needles

STITCH GUIDE

Garter Stitch (worked flat):
All rows: K all sts.

Single Rib (worked in the round):
All rnds: *P1, k1, rep from *.

ABBREVIATIONS

CO – cast on
BO – bind off
k – knit
k2tog – k 2 sts together (1 st dec)
st(s) – stitch(es)
rnd – round
beg – beginning
dec – decrease
incr – increase
p – purl
p2tog – p 2 sts together (1 st dec)
pm – place marker
pu – pick up
rep – repeat
rem – remain
rnd – round
RS – right side
sl – slip
sm – slip marker
ssk – slip slip knit (1 st dec)
WS – wrong side

DIRECTIONS

Back
Using long-tail method and US 8 (5 mm) needles, CO 80 (88, 96, 104, 112) sts.

Work in Garter Stitch until piece measures 22 (24, 26, 27, 28) inches from CO edge.
BO all sts.

Front
Work as for back until piece measures 3 1/2 (3 1/2, 4, 4, 4) inches from CO edge.

Next row (RS): BO 30 (30, 32, 34, 36) sts, k to end. 50 (58, 64, 70, 76) sts.

Next row (WS): K 50 (58, 64, 70, 76) sts, CO 30 (30, 32, 34, 36) sts. 80 (88, 96, 104, 112) sts.

Turn work and cont working front in Garter Stitch until piece measures 18 (20, 22, 23, 24) inches from CO edge.

Shape Crewneck
K across 33 (36, 40, 43, 46) sts, join new yarn and BO 14 (16, 16, 18, 20) sts for neck, k 33 (36, 40, 43, 46) sts to end. 33 (36, 40, 43, 46) sts rem for each shoulder.

Neck Decrease Row 1: On first shoulder, k to last 5 sts, k2tog twice k1. On second shoulder, k1, ssk twice, k to end. 2 sts decreased on each shoulder. 31 (34, 38, 41, 44) sts each shoulder.

Work Neck Decrease Row 1 again. 29 (32, 36, 39, 42) sts each shoulder.

Neck Decrease Row 2: On first shoulder, k to last sts, k2tog, k1. On second shoulder, k1, ssk, k to end. 1 st decreased on each shoulder. 28 (31, 35, 38, 41) sts each shoulder.
Work 1 row even, knitting all sts with no decreasing.

Repeat above two rows (Neck Decrease Row 2, then even row) once more. 27 (30, 34, 37, 40) sts each shoulder.

Work even in Garter Stitch until armholes measure same as back to the shoulders - entire piece should measure 22 (24, 26, 27, 28) inches from CO edge.
BO all sts.

Seam shoulders using a horizontal invisible garter stitch seam.

Crewneck Neckband
Starting at shoulder with smaller needle and RS facing, PU and knit 56 (60, 64, 70, 74) sts. Join in the round and PM. Work in Single Rib stitch for 8 rounds. BO loosely, in pattern.

SEAMING
Sew remaining side seams using a vertical edge garter stitch seam. Leave a 9 1/2 (10, 10 1/2, 11, 12) inch opening for arm hole on each side.

ARM OPENINGS
Starting at underarm with smaller needle and RS facing, pick up and knit 80 (84, 90, 94, 102) sts around arm opening.

Work in Single Rib stitch for 8 rounds. BO loosely, in pattern. Repeat for second arm opening.

FINISHING
Using tapestry needle, weave in ends.

BLOCKING
Soak using your favorite no-rinse wash in lukewarm water for 15-20 minutes, gently lay garment out and shape. Dry flat.

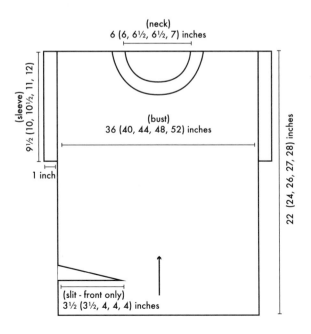

ZERO

DESIGN NOTES

Wear this modern, minimalist tank on its own or as a layering piece. Zero is worked seamlessly in the round from the bottom up to the armholes. Shaping on the front and back are knit flat as noted; straps are knit separately and then sewn on. Top is to be worn with positive ease of 1.5-2 inches as noted below.

SIZES

XS (S, M, L, XL)
To Fit Bust: 36 (40, 44, 48, 52) inches

FINISHED MEASUREMENTS

Finished Bust Circumference: 38 (42, 45, 49, 54) inches
Sample shown with positive ease of approximately 1.75 inches.

YARN

Wool and the Gang Crazy Sexy Wool in Space Black
(Super Bulky, 100% Peruvian wool; 87 yards per 200 g ball)
2 (2, 3, 3, 4) balls
174 (174, 261, 261, 348) yards

NEEDLES

US 19 (15 mm) 29" circular needles
(or size needed to obtain gauge)

NOTIONS

Stitch marker
Tapestry needle

GAUGE

4 inches = 5 1/2 sts and 9 rows in St st on size 19 (15 mm) needles, unblocked

STITCH GUIDE

Single Rib (worked in the round)
All rnds: *P1, k1, rep from *.

Stockinette Stitch (worked in the round)
All rnds: K all sts.

Stockinette Stitch (worked flat):
Row 1 (RS): K all sts.
Row 2 (WS): P all sts.

ABBREVIATIONS

CO – cast on
BO – bind off
k – knit
st(s) – stitch(es)
rnd – round
beg – beginning
dec – decrease
est – established
inc – increase
p – purl
patt – pattern
pm – place marker
rep – repeat
rem – remaining
rnd(s) – round
RS – right side
st(s) – stitch(es)
sl – slip
sm – slip marker
WS – wrong side

DIRECTIONS

Using long-tail method and US 19 (15 mm) needles, CO 52 (58, 62, 68, 74) sts. Join for working in the round and PM, taking care not to twist sts.

Work Single Rib stitch pattern for 4 rnds total.
Begin working Stockinette Stitch in the rnd until piece measures 13 (13, 14, 14, 15) inches from CO edge.

Begin Single Rib Patt:

Rnd 1 (dec): P1, k22 (26, 28, 30, 34) sts, p1, k26 (28, 30, 34, 36) sts, k2tog. 51 (57, 61, 67, 73) sts.

Rnd 2: P1, k22 (26, 28, 30, 34) sts, p1, k1, p1, k23 (25, 27, 31, 33), k2.

Rnd 3: P1, k22 (26, 28, 30, 34) sts, p1, k1, p1, k1, p1, k21 (23, 25, 29, 31), p1, k1.

Rnd 4: Work single rib patt across all sts. Turn work, keeping rem sts on needle.

You will now begin working front and back flat separately as foll:

BACK

Row 1 (WS): BO 1 st, work next 23 (26, 28, 31, 34) sts in single rib patt as est, k2tog. Slip unworked 25 (28, 30, 33, 36) sts to scrap yarn or stitch holders to be worked later for the Front. 24 (27, 29, 32, 35) sts rem on needles for Back. Turn work.
Row 2 (RS): BO 1 st, work 21 (24, 26, 29, 33) sts in single rib patt as est, k2tog. 22 (25, 27, 30, 33) sts rem.
Row 3 (WS): BO 1 st, work 19 (22, 24, 27, 30) sts in single rib patt as est, k2tog. 20 (23, 25, 28, 31) sts rem.
BO all sts in pattern.

FRONT

Return 25 (28, 30, 33, 36) sts to needles and attach yarn.
Row 1 (WS): BO 1 st, work next 22 (25, 27, 30, 33) sts in single rib patt as est, k2tog. 23 (26, 28, 31, 34) sts rem.
Row 2 (RS): BO 1 st, work 20 (23, 25, 28, 31) sts in single rib patt as est, k2tog. 21 (24, 26, 29, 32) sts rem.
Row 3 (WS): BO 1 st, work 18 (21, 23, 26, 29) sts in single rib patt as est, k2tog. 19 (22, 24, 27, 30) sts rem.
BO all sts in pattern.

STRAPS (Make 2)

Using long-tail method and US 19 (15 mm) needles, CO 5 sts. Work flat as follows:
Row 1 (RS): Slip 1 st, *K1, p1, rep from * to end.
Row 2 (WS): Slip 1 st, *P1, k1, rep from * to end.
Rep rows 1 & 2 until strap measures 13 (14, 15, 15.5, 16) in from CO edge.
BO all sts in pattern.

SEAMING

Seam shoulder straps to front and back by holding the ends of the straps on the inside of the body at the corners of each BO section. Seam horizontally along the BO/CO edges. Secure and fasten off.

FINISHING

Using tapestry needle, weave in ends.

BLOCKING

I do not recommend blocking this particular yarn/garment. If blocking is needed, lay out garment and shape to desired shape and dimensions. Gently spritz with water in a spray bottle until damp, but not soaking wet. Allow to dry completely.

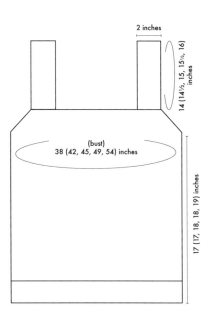

EQUINOX

DESIGN NOTES
Equinox is a pair of stirrup thigh-high yoga socks and they are made of 100% cashmere. These socks are seamless and worked in the round from the bottom up and exude pure style and luxury. Cozy up in these all winter long.

SIZES
S (M, L)
To Fit Instep/Foot Circumference: 8 (9, 10) inches

FINISHED MEASUREMENTS
Approximately 8 (9, 10) inch foot circumference and 25 inches long from heel to top of leg opening, with a 16 (17, 18) inch leg opening circumference

YARN
Bijou Spun Xanadu in Black (Lt Fingering; 100% Mongolian Cashmere; 400 yds per 2 oz hank)
2 (2, 2) hanks
800 (800, 800) yards

NEEDLES
US 2 (2.75 mm) 32 inch circular needles (or longer) for magic loop or 8 inch double pointed needles
(or size needed to obtain gauge)

NOTIONS
Stitch markers (2 in contrasting colors)
Tapestry needle

GAUGE
4 inches = 32 sts and 40 rows in St st on US 2 (2.75 mm) needles

ABBREVIATIONS
CO – cast on
BO – bind off
k – knit
st(s) – stitch(es)
rnd – round
beg – beginning
inc – increase
p – purl
pm – place marker
rep – repeat
rnd – round
st st – stockinette stitch
kfb – knit into the front and back of the same stitch (one stitch increased)

DIRECTIONS FOR SOCKS (Make 2)

Foot

Using long-tail method on US 2 needles, CO 64 (72, 80) sts. Join to work in the round, taking care not to twist sts. PM to mark beginning of round.

*K2, p2, rep from * for 8 rnds.

Next rnd: K around until piece measures 3 inches from CO edge.

Heel Opening

Next rnd: BO 32 (36, 40) sts, k to end of rnd. 32 (36, 40) rem on the needles.

Next rnd: CO 32 (36, 40) sts, k to end of rnd. Join to work in the round. 64 (72, 80) sts.

Leg

K all rnds for 2 inches. Begin leg increases as follows:

Rnd 1: K 32 (36, 40) sts, place contrasting marker to mark middle of rnd, k to end of rnd.

Rnds 2-6: K all sts.

Rnd 7 (inc rnd): Kfb, k to middle of rnd marker, kfb, k to end or rnd. 2 sts increased. 66 (74, 82) sts.

Repeat Rnds 2-7 above 31 more times. 128 (136, 144) sts.

*K2, p2, rep from * for 2 inches.

BO in pattern using Jeny Staiman's Surprisingly Stretchy Bind-Off, or your favorite stretchy bind off method.

FINISHING

Cut yarn, leaving a 6-8 in tail. Using tapestry needle, weave in ends.

If socks don't stay up, fold top hem in half and use matching thread to hand-sew in a length of non-roll elastic, measured to fit your thigh.

BLOCKING

Soak using your favorite no-rinse wash for 20 minutes, gently lay out and shape socks. Dry flat.

LANEY

DESIGN NOTES

Laney is a must-knit, with its simple, modern shape and interesting stitch pattern. The Lateral Braid stitch (also knows as the Estonian or Vikkel Braid) will turn your knitting in a new direction and is the featured design element in the center of this cowl. A quick knit, Laney is worked seamlessly in the round with the yarn held double.

SIZES
One size

FINISHED MEASUREMENTS
60 inch circumference and 8 inches wide

YARN
Rowan Big Wool in Glum (Bulky; 100% Merino wool; 80 yds per 100 g ball)
5 balls
400 yards

NEEDLES
US 19 (16 mm) 24 inch circular needles
(or size needed to obtain gauge)

NOTIONS
Stitch markers
Tapestry needle

GAUGE
4 inches = 6 sts and 8 rows in Seed Stitch on US 19 (16 mm) needles with yarn held double

STITCH GUIDE
Seed Stitch
Rnd 1: *K1, p1; rep from * to end of rnd.
Rnd 2: *P1, k1; rep from * to end of rnd.
Rep rnds 1 and 2 for pattern.

Stockinette Stitch
All rnds: K all sts.

Lateral Braid
(Video tutorial on www.jengeigley.com)
Using cable cast on, CO 1 st onto left-hand needle.
*Ktbl into second st on left-hand needle. Do not slide st off needle. K first st on left-hand needle. Slide both sts off needle onto right-hand needle. Sl the last worked st from the right needle back to the left needle. Rep from * to last st in rnd. K last st, then pass the second st on right needle over.

ABBREVIATIONS
CO – cast on
BO – bind off
k – knit
st(s) – stitch(es)
rnd – round
beg – beginning
inc – increase
ktbl – knit through back loop
patt – pattern
p – purl
pm – place marker
rep – repeat
rnd – round
st – stitch
sts – stitches
st st – stockinette stitch
sl – slip

DIRECTIONS

Holding yarn double and using long-tail method on US 19 needles, CO 90 sts. Join to work in the round, taking care not to twist sts. PM to mark beginning of round.

Work Seed Stitch for 5 rnds.

Work Stockinette Stitch for 3 rnds.

Work Lateral Braid stitch for 1 rnd.

Work Stockinette Stitch for 3 rnds.

Work Seed Stitch for 4 rnds.

BO all sts in pattern, loosely.

FINISHING

Cut yarn, leaving a 6-8 inch tail. Using tapestry needle, weave in ends.

BLOCKING

Lay out garment and shape to desired shape and dimensions. Gently spritz with water in a spray bottle until damp, but not soaking wet. Allow to dry completely.

RESOURCES

SOURCES

YARN

Bijou Basin Ranch
www.bijoubasinranch.com

Blue Sky Fibers
www.blueskyfibers.com

Briggs and Little
www.briggsandlittle.com

Lux Adorna Knits
www.luxadornaknits.com

Rowan Yarns
www.knitrowan.com

Manos del Uruguay
www.fairmountfibers.com

Spud & Chloë by Blue Sky Fibers
www.spudandchloe.com

Wool and the Gang
www.woolandthegang.com

NEEDLES & SUPPLIES

Knitter's Pride
www.knitterspride.com

Fringe Supply Co.
www.fringesupplyco.com

Ritual Oracle
www.lovekp.bigcartel.com

ABBREVIATIONS

beg	beginning
BO	bind off
CO	cast on
cont	continue
dec	decrease
DPN	double pointed needle
est	established
foll	following
in	inches
inc	increase
k	knit
k2tog	knit 2 together (1 stitch decreased)
kf&b	knit into front and back of stitch (one stitch increased)
ktbl	knit through back loop
kw	knitwise
mm	millimeters
m1r	make one right
m1l	make one left
p	purl
p2tog	purl 2 sts together (1 stitch decreased)
patt	pattern
pm	place marker
pu	pick up
rem	remaining
rep	repeat
rnd(s)	round(s)
RS	right side
sl	slip
sm	slip marker
ssk	slip slip knit (1 stitch decreased)
st(s)	stitch(es)
st st	stockinette stitch
tog	together
WS	wrong side
yo	yarn over

SPECIAL TECHNIQUES

LONG TAIL CAST ON

Begin with a long tail, roughly three times the width of your finished piece of knitting. Leaving your estimated length of yarn for the long tail, make a slip knot. Place the slip knot on one needle and gently pull the yarn tails to tighten. Hold needle in your right hand with the tip of the needle pointing to the left. Using your left hand, grasp the two yarn ends below the slip knot. With your left thumb pressing against your left forefinger, move your thumb and forefinger through the space between the two strands. The long tail should be lying over your thumb and the working yarn over your forefinger. Spread your thumb and forefinger apart and lower the needle so that the yarn makes a V between the thumb and forefinger. Hold both tails tightly against your palm with your ring and pinky finger. With the needle in your right hand, pass the needle under the yarn around the thumb, over the top of the yarn around the forefinger, and back through the yarn around the thumb. Pull the thumb out from the yarn loop and pull gently on the yarn tails to tighten stitch. Repeat these steps until you have cast on the required number of stitches.

PICKING UP STITCHES

Slide knitting needle into an existing stitch, then slide your other needle underneath (into the stitch as if to knit.) Pull the stitch through. You now have a new stitch on your needle. Repeat until you have picked up the number of stitches specified in the pattern.

MATTRESS STITCH – VERTICAL

Thread yarn 3 to 4 times the length of your finished edge onto a tapestry needle. Lay pieces to be sewn flat with edges next to each other, with the right sides facing you. Line up the rows/stitches. Insert a tapestry needle between the first and second stitches in the first row. Slide the tapestry needle under two rows, then bring it back to the front between the first and second stitch of the row. Starting on the opposite end, work under two rows again and repeat, zig-zagging from side to side. Stitch under the strands that correspond directly to the other side without skipping rows. Keep the seam elastic by working loosely, then pulling seam stitches gently after working a few inches.

VERTICAL SEAM – GARTER STITCH

Thread yarn 3 to 4 times the length of your finished edge onto a tapestry needle. Line up the two edges to be seamed, with the right sides facing you. Insert the yarn needle into the top loop (∩) on one side, then in the bottom loop (U) of the corresponding stitch on the other side. Continue to alternate in this way, working loosely, then pulling seam stitches gently after working a few inches.

HORIZONTAL SEAM – GARTER STITCH

Take your two knitted pieces and lay them end to end, right side up. Thread yarn 3 to 4 times the length of your finished edge onto a tapestry needle. Start one row in from the bind-off/cast-on edge of one of your pieces and locate the first purl bump. Using the tip of your needle, follow the line of the bump to where it goes under another purl bump and insert your needle along that path. Insert needle under the first purl bump on your other piece and do the same. Stitch back into your first piece and insert needle under the same purl bump you used before, but going the opposite direction. Continue to alternate in this way, working loosely, then pulling seam stitches gently after working a few inches. Essentially, this will look like a duplicate purl stitch.

LATERAL BRAID

Also, known as the Estonian Braid or Vikkel Braid, this stitch creates a braid that runs horizontally across your work. Using cable cast on, Cast on 1 stitch onto left-hand needle. *Knit through the back loop into second stitch on left-hand needle. Do not slide stitch off needle. Knit first stitch on left-hand needle. Slide both stitches off needle onto right-hand needle. Slip the last worked stitch from the right needle back to the left needle. Repeat from * to last stitch in the round. Knit the last stitch, then pass the second stitch on right needle over.

Visit www.jengeigley.com for video tutorials of these techniques.

ACKNOWLEDGEMENTS

I would like to personally thank the following people for their support in the making of this book:

Stefanie Goodwin-Ritter for being the absolute best technical editor a girl could ask for. For months, this project was our little secret and behind the scenes you made everything work. Thank you for not only caring about the math and the measurements, but for being a great friend too. You are the most patient person on earth.

Joelle Blanchard for being the wind beneath my wings. You are my favorite co-conspirator; my muse. Every single thing you do is magic. You somehow make working on both sides of the camera seem effortless. So beautiful, every damn time. Thank you for taking my pile of knits and my small ideas and running with it. You always get my vision, and then take it to a place that's ten times cooler than I could have imagined. Thanks for being my fellow daydreamer and go-getter.

Joey Leaming for saying 'yes' to this project again. And always letting us crash your studio/living space, wherever that happens to be. Thank you for the ever-important background music/soundtrack, and for pulling absolute magic out of thin air and making this book look so cool. You have such innate talent and a kind, relaxed way about you that makes you so fun to work with. (We didn't even use one light.)

You two are my dream team – thank you all for making my hand-knit dreams come to life in the most beautiful way. Twice.

Chantell Moody for coming back to Des Moines and carving out the time to do this. Beauty radiates from your soul and it was so wonderful to work with you.

Valerie Sanders for bringing your killer cool style to this project. You are a beauty – inside and out – and it's an honor to have you grace these pages.

Chantell, Joelle and Valerie – you all rocked this so hard, just by being you. Seeing your photos for the first time made me cry happy tears.

Erin Hogan for being a friend, an editor and a proofreader at any time of day or night. I am the luckiest to have you as a friend and I definitely owe you dinner at Orlando's.

Erica Carnes and **Jessica Miller** at **Hill Vintage and Knits**, my most favorite entrepreneurial yarn store owners and knitXmidwest comrades. Hill is my yarn store home and I adore you two babes.

Thank you to my local knitting gang: **Emily, Nichole, Melissa, Sarah, Taylor, Jenni, Joshua Benet, Darcy, Alexis, Nikki, Heidi, Amanda, Amy, Robyn.** An extra special shout-out to my Reed's Hollow Taco-Tuesday-on-a-Wednesday-night knitters who watched me knit most of the things in this book. (Also, thank you to the Reed's staff for always letting us stay and knit until midnight. And for the delicious tacos.)

Emily Elliott for my daily everything. You understand all the facets of my life and listen to my weird ideas over and over again, without a single complaint. When I was indecisive, you were there. You are magnetic, genuine and wonderful and your support never ends. Thank you for being there every step of the way. Every single day.

Bethany Arganbright for being a fantastic friend. Thank you for keeping it real, bringing things back to basics and helping me hone in on the right name/concept for this thing.

Kristi Prokopiak and **Jamaica Edgell**, for making my house a pit-stop on the #GTFONYC roadtrip. Our late-night talks are gold. You both continue to be a huge long-distance inspiration to me from wherever you are in the world.

Steven Berg, **Missy Ridley** and the **StevenBe gang** for your unending love and support this past year. Thank you for letting me sleep in the fiber loft and for our adventures in NYC. Dreams come true. You are an inspiration and I love you guys from the bottom of my heart.

Fred and **Karen Posniak** for inviting me to dinner and then taking me to the top of the Empire State Building. You two are amazing friends.

Gaye Gillespie (GGmadeit) for finding Weekend and then sharing it with the knitting world. Thank you for being my best new knitting pal. You are a constant light in the world.

My heartfelt thanks to my **crafty internet friends**, far and wide, who have been there all along with support and words of encouragement via the magical world of blogs, emails, Instagram photos, Ravelry projects and Facebook groups.

A huge thank you to the kind people at **Bijou Basin Ranch, Blue Sky Fibers, Briggs and Little, Lux Adorna Knits, Rowan Yarns, Manos del Uruguay, Spud & Chloë** and **Wool and the Gang**. Without your yarn support, this book wouldn't be possible.

Mom and **Dad**. Thank you for supporting all my weird hobbies and allowing me to hide out in my room to draw, paint and listen to music. Mom – thanks for teaching me to sew, cross-stitch and crochet. Dad – thanks for the Led Zeppelin, the Queen and all the good rock and roll. Your unbeatable pep talks still play in my head after all these years.

And last but not least, thank you to my awesomely wild and wonderful family: **Bo, Lotus** and **Bowie**. This might have been the most transitional, crazy, beautiful year we've ever had. I love you guys more fiercely than ever. I could not follow my dreams and manage to write a book without your sweet faces in my life every day. You put the smile on my face and the beat in my heart. I love you more than knitting.

AT A GLANCE

GWEN
SCARF/COWL
PAGE 84

LEO
SUPER SCARF
PAGE 88

CERES
TANK
PAGE 92

AURA
HAT
PAGE 108

MOONSTONE
SWEATER
PAGE 112

ZERO
TANK
PAGE 116

ERIS
COWL
PAGE 96

JESSA
SWEATER
PAGE 100

CHILL
FINGERLESS GLOVES
PAGE 104

EQUINOX
THIGH-HIGH SOCKS
PAGE 120

LANEY
COWL
PAGE 124

ABOUT THE AUTHOR

Jen Geigley lives and knits in Des Moines, Iowa, with her husband and two children. Known for her clean, modern designs, Jen has an appreciation for simple knits that are easy to wear. Her designs have been published in *Knit Simple Magazine, Noro Magazine, Knitsy Magazine, Love of Knitting Magazine, Rowan's Online Publications* and she has self-published knitwear patterns online since 2010. In 2016, she wrote and self-published her first book *Weekend: Simple, Modern Knits*. Jen is passionate about sharing her love of knitting by teaching beginner knitting classes to adults and children at local schools and workshops, and loves to knit with her daughter. Originally trained in the arts, she creates her own sketches, illustrations, schematics and graphic design work. In her spare time, she enjoys watching Quentin Tarantino movies, going to concerts and listening to all genres of music.

Website: www.jengeigley.com
Blog: www.heyjenrenee.com

Made in United States
Troutdale, OR
12/11/2023

15716798R00086